Make Peace with Anxiety

Manage the Good, Bad, and Out of Control

Alivette Vigo

D1153809

ISBN: paperback 979-8-9852923-4-3

ISBN: ebook 979-8-9852923-8-1

Dedication

To my lovely daughter, because you make me feel young, creative, and fun. Thank you for being such a beautiful person.

To my family, ex-husband, and the friends who supported me throughout the healing and writing process. You know I mean well, and I love you all.

To the person to whom I do not get to express what I wrote. I don't judge you for taking such a final decision. I pray that you rest in peace.

Pledge Invitation

Take the pledge to prioritize yourself

The pledge is your commitment to improving your mental health and practice self-love.

Join me and all the people who have pledged to put themselves first and act by going to:

alivettev.authorchannel.co
Print, sign and place the pledge in an area you see every day.

Introduction

In the eyes of many, I am successful. This is my reality today, but it has not always been that way. Unless I mention it, you probably wouldn't know that I manage an anxiety disorder, have experienced several panic attacks and cycles of depression, and have been diagnosed with post-traumatic stress disorder (PTSD). I will share some of my experiences throughout the book, but please understand that we all experience mental struggles differently. Some people are able to manage it well; others find it hard to control, and therefore it affects their daily lives negatively. Your situation does not have to match mine. There is not a life comparison; we are all unique in this world. However, the one thing we should agree on is that mental wellness is essential to everyone.

Collectively, we need to support one another. We put pressure on ourselves to create the most perfect, successful life our society has conditioned us to think we need. Whether we fail or succeed, we still find ourselves anxious or depressed sometimes, and for some, all the time.

Anxiety disorders and depression are more common than we, as a society, admit. Thankfully, we can all relate to and help one another because we all share the human condition. You are not alone if you are struggling with anxiety or depression or both. Or you might want to help someone who does. Like any other medical issue, mental struggles can be managed effectively with early detection, an action plan, and a support system. I would like to say that I naturally figured this out, but that is hardly the case. It took me a long time of experiencing, learning, accepting, and treating myself with kindness to gracefully nurture my anxiety into coexistence. Now that I have achieved this healthy level of coexistence, I am sharing it with you.

My early twenties looked a lot like this: a mother, a wife, a volunteer for various charities, an active-duty military service member with an organized, clean house—all while also looking attractive. I checked every box of the adult societal expectations list to the best of my abilities, and my personality added more boxes, because I have always been an overachiever. I should also mention that I am a very emotional, passionate, and empathetic person. There was nothing wrong with any of that, except that I was not including my mental health in the mix. In my life up to this point, anxiety was like a weighing scale that would help me measure risk versus reward. Feelings of anxiety, mixed with other emotions like excitement, help me excel.

I was prepared for every event or challenge. My performances were usually superb and nothing less. As time passed, the same level of anxiety that used to help me started to break me emotionally. I did not consider myself a perfectionist, but looking back, I totally was. I put a lot of pressure on myself, had many fears, and consequently developed some stress-related physical symptoms.

I can't particularly pinpoint when I lost the ability to control my anxiety and use it to my benefit. It could have been the desire of being better, doing more, or pursuing the illusion of perfection. As I tried harder, anxiety started to turn on me. Now, I understand that was my body's way of telling me that I was living in a way that I could no longer sustain. I was burning out in every way. I was not getting the message, so I kept pushing myself because that was all I knew, and it had proved effective time after time. Throughout the years, I experienced moments of happiness and joy; yet, I also had cycles of intense anxiety and depression, manifesting in the forms of stomach pains, tension headaches, lack of sleep and appetite—or overeating and sleeping—negative thoughts, and hair loss. I was in denial; this denial came from the lack of knowledge, the stigma associated with mental disorders, the shame of thinking that something could be wrong with me, and the fear of what would people think. Was I a fake? Was this normal? And what is normal, anyway?

Anxiety is a normal feeling like many others we experience. However, if you find yourself constantly worrying, choosing between the worst of all the possible scenarios, affected by the things you can't control, or unable to sleep because you sent an email with a typo to your child's teacher and now feel like an inadequate parent, then we need to look at what can we do to help you live a better quality of life. Sometimes anxiety and depression can be managed with a wellness plan that can assist you until you are more relaxed and in control of your emotions, created in collaboration with a qualified medical professional. Other times, you may need reoccurring treatment, and that is perfectly okay. This is a simple concept, yet it has been twisted by the mental stigmas society has created. Let's face it, the only reason there is stigma here is because we make one. We are not crazy because we are seeking to improve our mental health. You would not hesitate to go to the doctor if you suspected you had diabetes, right? If you are in the early stages of diabetes, you may control it by changing your diet and exercise. Furthermore, if your body needs insulin, you'd take medication by pill or even injection as prescribed with no hesitation. Why should anxiety or any mental struggles be treated any different?

The purpose of this book is to encourage you to make your mental health a priority. The mind is very intricate. Traumatic events and family health history have been tied to mental illnesses, but there may be other unknown contributors. According to the Mayo Clinic nonprofit organization, the underlying causes of anxiety disorders are still not yet understood; however, early or continuous management of anxiety can help prevent other mental and physical conditions from developing. I can't emphasize enough the importance of fighting the stigma associated with mental struggles, promoting a healthy lifestyle, living consciously, and taking initiative toward wellness.

Important note! Suffering from anxiety and depression is not the same as feeling suicidal. If you or someone you know are experiencing suicidal thoughts, contact the National Suicide Prevention Lifeline or dial 911 immediately. If you are not in the United States, call your local police or medical emergency department.

Contents

Chapter 1

Anxiety Range

Every emotion serves a specific purpose in our lives. This is what sets us apart from robots and mannequins. Emotions are neither good nor bad; they assist us in processing moments, situations, and anything our minds naturally react to. Emotions intensify our experiences and should be expressed in a healthy manner. If you are happy because you adopted a puppy, then celebrate—smile, feel the love, kiss the puppy. If you are sad because you lost a loved one, cry and grieve. When you acknowledge and process the emotions, you are practicing good mental health. However, if an emotion starts manifesting intensively, producing negative thoughts, affecting your daily performances, or leading to an unhealthy behavior or physical pain, you need to speak up and seek help. Easier said than done, right? When you are experiencing mind struggles, the last thing you probably want is to speak up and be judged. However, remember that there should be no shame for expressing how you feel, and it is your responsibility to take care of yourself. No one should live being sad, in pain, anxious, or depressed all the time. Yes, these situations do happen, but we are meant to overcome, move forward, and live the best life possible.

Dealing with anxiety as a child was much easier for me than as an adult. I had a very decisive mind, almost fearless—regardless of the outcome. My recollections of childhood are vivid. I describe my younger self as resilient with the occasional physical insecurities and need for attention. I grew up in a farm-like environment with pigs and chickens, plenty of vegetation, flowers, and fruit that I could eat on the spot. Being an only child running around with a vast imagination, anxiety was a friend of mine. I would spot grapefruits on a tall tree, and my gut feelings would help me decide whether the risk was worth the prize. My thought process was something like this: "If I get up the tree, I could fall. Yet logically, I am a good climber, and if I fall, landing on the grass probably won't hurt as much." As I climbed to reach the grapefruits, the anxious feeling of getting the task done without falling kept me alert. Being able to grab the fruit from the top of the tree to eat with no assistance was exciting, and the reward was delicious.

Around eight years old, I practiced karate and did so for a total of six years. Right before every tournament, anxiety would set in. The nerves made me look and perform sharp. I won many medals and trophies, and most fights were with boys! In 1992, I won a Grand Champion belt in the Puerto Rico open challenge competition and was featured in a local newspaper's sports section. Winning was exciting, and I looked intimidating even though I was nervous on the inside. In martial arts, you never show an opponent that you are scared; you show them that you are ready to fight. Ironically, this sport first exposed me to meditation and forms (katas), two wonderful activities about relaxing and releasing. Yet, the fiercely competitive aspect of the sport caused me to relate showing emotions with weakness. At this age, aside from sports, I also perceived from people in general that expressing feelings was a vulnerability. No one wants to hear doubt or negative emotions from a kid because of the perception that kids don't know anything about life yet.

Throughout out my whole academic school experience, I was a straight A student. I would study the night before every exam, even if I knew the material, because anxiety would remind me that there could be something I missed, and I wanted to do well. I graduated with a high school diploma and accounting clerk vocational certificate the same year I joined the United States Navy. I accomplished all of this while also working a part-time job and recovering from a broken heart caused by a toxic teenage romantic relationship. You could say the level of anxiety I experienced was normal for the situations described.

I am not sure if I even knew what anxiety was since it felt more like justified recurring worries or fears. I do not know if seeking help could have prevented the anxiety disorder, but it would have definitely helped me understand and manage better. Looking back, I recognize the loneliness and hurdles I went through attempting to deal with anxiety on my own, despite having access to resources and people who cared. It was probably pride or shame that stopped me. Since we dismiss or fear what we do not understand, education is the best place to start.

Anxiety.org defines anxiety as "the mind and body's reaction to stressful, dangerous, or unfamiliar situations. It's the sense of uneasiness, distress, or dread you feel before a significant event. A certain level of anxiety helps us stay alert and aware, but for those suffering from an anxiety disorder, it feels far from normal—it can be completely debilitating."

I am not a doctor, but here is my personal definition: Anxiety is the feeling that takes away my confidence, frustrates me, and makes me physically sick. Anxiety was a wild animal in my mind that would terrorize every effort I put into creating a good, quality life. It sabotaged me until I realized that it needed attention, love, and understanding. Anxiety still exists and will continue, but I managed to domesticate it, therefore making peace with it.

I presume you are not a doctor, either, and are trying to find information you can relate to. Perhaps you can come up with your own definition of anxiety based on how anxiety has affected you.

The good news is you do not have to do any of this work alone. There are many professionals and resources available to assist you.

I would like to clarify that seeking resources or seeing a mental help professional does not mean you will automatically get medicated or that your children will be taken away. The number one comment I hear from people when I suggest seeking mental help is that they don't want to get medicated. They may also get defensive and state they don't need a doctor because they are strong-minded or their anxiety is not that bad. I understand, as I too used to say the same thing when people started picking up I was tense. I also did not know how to start the conversation. However, the way to start any awkward, embarrassing, or difficult conversation is to start it just like that. As uncomfortable as this conversation may be, open the conversation with: *I don't know why I feel this way, but____; I am feeling uneasy, down, or I am embarrassed to say____*. Another way to deal with the awkwardness is scheduling an appointment with a health professional and letting them ask you questions or filling out the background questionnaire. If you can express it all, then do it. If you are like me, who cries easily when emotional, then write it on a paper and hand it over. I have done this more than once, and it has saved me time and energy. Communicating how you feel is the starting point of finding solutions and releasing what has been build up inside. Have compassion for yourself and honor your feelings; you deserve a good life free of worries, sadness, and fear.

Ideally, evaluating mental health would be as simple as asking self-assessment questions on feelings and moods, but there is more to it than that. There are other areas to consider. Do you have other medical problems that may trigger anxiety or depression? Some physical and mental health issues may cause anxiety as an indication that something else is going on or may be secondary to the health issue. Chronic back and neck pain has caused me anxiety. I consider myself a physically active person despite my medical conditions. When my body hurts, anxiety creeps in to remind me of all the stuff I have to do, and the pain is an inconvenience that slows me down. The thought of my body breaking down when I am still young is frustrating. Are you taking a medication that has anxiety or depression as a side effect? If so, you need to call your doctor to discuss the medication and the possibility of changing to a more appropriate dose or to a different medication. It is very important that you do not change or stop the medications on your own. Always consult your doctor!

Do you have family history of mental health issues? This does not mean that you will automatically get an inherited mental health issue that runs in family, but you are more likely to than someone who does not have a family history of it. As a side note, our families play a big role in mental health since the environments we grew up in, the beliefs we were taught, the situations we experienced, and other factors contribute to our mental development. It is worth mentioning again that mental struggles can still occur even if you had the "perfect" childhood or if you are living a good life.

What are your anxiety symptoms? When did they start? How frequently do they occur? Are you able to spot a pattern? Or are they symptoms occurring at random, unpredictable times? Often, we ignore symptoms hoping they will just go away on their own. Symptoms are our body's way to let us know something is happening, and we need to pay attention.

Have you experienced trauma and not spoken to anyone about it? If you have, please make an appointment as soon as you can with a mental health professional. There is no reason why you need to go through anything emotionally alone. The healing process may be hard but it is necessary. Speaking about it is the first step. I learned this the hard way. There were situations in my life I never spoke about because I was in unfriendly environments or because I had been suppressing the emotions to forget them—only to have those emotions released in the form of panic attacks pushing me to deal with them at unpredictable times, years or even decades later.

Are you experiencing a drug, alcohol, or medication withdrawal? These substances can cause or worsen anxiety. Consult a doctor for help on quitting. A doctor will direct you, monitor your overall health, and act as an accountability partner. When I was in the military, I was treated with a muscle relaxer for an injury that at the time was not properly diagnosed. Every time I attempted to stop the medication, my level of anxiety increased extensively. In other words, I was addicted to muscle relaxer.

When you meet with a mental health professional, you will want to have all this information handy because your doctor only has a limited time with you, and what you say helps them best assess and help you by developing a plan to move forward. If you feel you need more time with a professional, make a second appointment. If you are not satisfied with one professional, find another. Make sure you follow your intuition; if you feel you need a second opinion, go for it. People sometimes get discouraged from their first appointment because it was not what they expected. This difficulty may be solved by not creating any expectations and not thinking that you will be "fixed" in one visit. There is no "fix," but there is a process to wellness. Expecting a "fix" only creates more anxiety and impatience. A mental health issue should be looked at and treated seriously, not rushed, and remember to eliminate the stigma and always be kind toward yourself.

Call your doctor, research a medical professional in your area, or contact your health insurance for assistance finding a mental health professional. You also have the option of talking to non-mental health professionals such as a social worker, school counselor, spiritual adviser, family, friends, or an employee assistant program coordinator for support—but they are not to give you medical advice. Although the non-mental health professionals provide good support and resources, you need to see a doctor if your symptoms are hard to control and anxiety is interfering negatively in your work, relationships, and physical health.

Once you meet with a mental health professional, they may give you a psychological evaluation. You need to be very honest. Don't feel judged by your answers. Even if some of your thoughts or worries are irrational and you know it, you need to express them. The health professional can only help you to the extent you let them. Don't hold back. You have no shame telling your dentist you don't floss every day; perhaps you lie, but the dentist will know if this is true when you get checked. Unfortunately, a health professional can't see your mind, so it is up to you to tell as much as you can to get the best diagnosis and care. If you cry often because you are overwhelmed with life responsibilities, say it. If your stress is affecting you physically, say it. If you feel like a failure or can't find joy anymore doing the things you used to love, say it. You are not a bad person; you just need some help and guidance until you are able to manage your emotions effectively on your own. If you do get diagnosed with a mental disorder, that is okay. Many people live a successful life while managing their mental disorders. Like I mentioned before, mental struggles are more common than we, as society, admit. Luckily, we can learn, treat, and manage them so that we can live a wonderful, good-quality life.

Here are a few questions for a quick anxiety awareness check:

- Do you worry daily about different things going wrong? When you worry, do you experience any physical symptoms?
- Do you worry so frequently that it is affecting your relationships? Do people avoid telling you things because you worry too much?
- Do your worries keep you up at night?

- Do your worries and fears prevent you from doing things you would like to try? Karaoke? Applying for your dream job? Asking someone on a date?
- Are you unable to relax on your own or calm your stress without medication, alcohol, or any substance that can alter your mental equilibrium?
- Do you feel awfully uncomfortable around a lot of people, avoid attending social gatherings, or dislike meeting new people?
- Is your work performance affected by anxiety? For example: You are not able to participate in meetings or give presentations; you are visibly nervous and feel embarrassed by it; perhaps you don't present new ideas because you fear rejection.

Whether you answer yes or no to these questions, anxiety management is important. If you answered no to most of these questions, you are managing anxiety well, but I encourage you to continue learning about mental wellness and help others as you are able to. If you answered yes to most questions, raise your knowledge about mental health, learn anxiety coping skills, and meet with the appropriate health professionals to create a wellness plan.

Chapter 2

Mental Disorders

Not feeling in control of your own emotions is scary. When anxiety gets out of control, it leads to other mental disturbances. This is precisely why anxiety management is so important in your life. You want to maintain control of your emotions, not the other way around. Your daily routine should not include mental struggles. If you find yourself thinking repeatedly about images, situations, and thoughts that are not serving you in any way, there is a problem. If such thinking is turning into irrational fear and worries or they seem intense, exaggerated, or obsessive, affecting your daily performance or preventing you from performing at all, you need medical attention. If you are not able to control anxiety, recognize it, and begin to understand it so you can work on helping yourself feel better, remember that it is your responsibility to take care of your body and there is no shame in that.

The National Alliance on Mental Illness reports, "Anxiety disorders are the most common mental health concern in the United States." If you are diagnosed with an anxiety disorder, you need to have compassion for yourself and always approach your treatment from a place of love. I say this because you probably don't want to hear that you have a disorder—I sure did not! I did not understand the self-compassion concept until one night I found myself crying on the floor, hyperventilating, experiencing a panic attack. Since it was late at night and I was alone, I recorded myself on my iPhone. At that moment, looking at myself made me feel accompanied. Two days later, I watched the video and felt so much love for what I saw; it was the kind of love that is so tender I can only describe as if I was watching a baby girl desperately in need of nourishment, protection, and acceptance. It took a video of my own panic attack to open my eyes and heart to self-compassion. Seeing myself this way provided an instant feeling of deep self-love I did not know I was capable of. There is always more than one way to view anything, and the fact that I was able to take this panic attack and choose to see it with compassion and love is remarkable. I would like to say that every negative thought or emotion has been received gracefully, but that was hardly the case. I have experienced three intense panics attacks that I can remember, and the rest I have been able to stop from escalating with some wellness strategies I will mention in later chapters.

My very first intense panic attack occurred at work. I had been tense, frustrated, and anxious for months. One day, I was having a quarterly meeting with my boss and started to feel nerves in my stomach. There was something about the conversation I perceived as unjust, and I believe that was the trigger. Slowly, I felt short of breath while speaking and the tone of my voice changed. I excused myself to go to the restroom. On my way there, I felt my chest not expanding when inhaling; I was suffocating, and I needed immediate air. Needless to say, there was air all around me, yet I felt I could not breathe it in. A warm sensation covered my face and neck that soon felt burning hot. An urgent need to go outside took over; I felt desperate for the air and was hyperventilating. I ran toward the elevator. I could not speak; my face and blouse were wet, though. I did not know I was crying (according to coworkers, ugly crying). I was trying to hide from everyone, and the elevator took what seemed like one hundred years to open. Once I got out of the building, I speed-walked to a grassy area where I could feel myself breathing again, and slowly, my body started to calm down. At this point, I believe I was sitting or lying on the grass. I was not in control of what was happening, and worse, I could not stop it. Years of neglecting my mental struggles had finally caught up with me, and I could no longer ignore it.

My employer paid for eight stress management counseling sessions as part of the employment assistance program they offered. At first, I was stubborn about attending counseling with a psychologist because I felt like the employer was addressing me rather than the work environment. It did not matter what argument I made; the fact is that while I was working in a stressful environment, I was the only one who suffered a panic attack. Everyone else could manage their stress and anxiety levels, while I struggled.

Counseling turned out to be more valuable than I expected. It was not obvious at first, but after a few sessions I started seeing improvements. I started to understand better what I was going through and this time, I was facing it. To my surprise, I discovered there were more things in my mind that were bothering me, and some of the situations at work were triggering suppressed emotions. During therapy, situations from prior decades I had never dealt with came out. I had suppressed my feelings until my body just said, "Enough! You will deal with all of this now," and so I did. I pledged to put my mental health first so that I could manage my emotions better. A word of advice: Pay attention to your mental health before your body shakes you up into action, which could happen at an inconvenient location and at any time. Start today—the sooner you can work on your mental wellness, the better results you will get. Make the effort and be patient. Wellness practices work with time and consistency.

Intense anxiety should be evaluated for diagnosis and proper treatment. I had been diagnosed with general anxiety disorder in the past and attributed my "episodes" to it. However, as I kept opening up emotionally about my experiences, the PTSD diagnosis became more apparent. Within six months after the first panic attack, I experienced two more and, in between, frequent anxiety and depression cycles. For a while, I lived in fear of experiencing another panic attack at any moment, without warning. I was very scared of not having control or losing my mind. I kept going to therapy. Then I started taking medication and paying attention to how I felt around people and in various places and situations.

A normal range of anxiety is associated with mild nervousness, excitement, and some worry. When the anxiety is a disorder, diagnosis, treatment, and wellness practices are a must. For awareness purposes, I would like to mention a few common disorders:

Generalized anxiety disorder is hard for me to deny. During a certification exam, I was so worried about answering and reviewing every question that I ran out of time during the test and failed. The entire test, I could feel my heart beat, kept looking at the time, and even second-guessed if I should have typed my full first name or my nickname on the registration page. The second time I took the exam, I passed—but I did not sleep the night before, had stomach pain, and threw up in the parking lot when I arrived at the testing center. I should be able to take a test, as important as it may be, without getting physically ill. Generalized anxiety disorder takes the fears and worries way out of proportion.

Depression mood disorder causes persistent sadness and no interest in the things you normally do or like. I experience depression in cycles that have lasted between one to three months at a time. A feeling of sadness comes over me and stays for a while. I don't want to get out of bed or leave the house, I don't want to socialize, and I can't find joy or anything I like. I am still able to function for work and the everyday living tasks because I make myself do so. I still tend to isolate and look sad or mad (according to the people around me). During these low times, I do the bare minimum and one thing at a time to keep me going. My body feels heavy and I can easily sleep twelve to fourteen hours per day.

Panic disorders are pretty much recurring episodes of panic attacks. Everyone's experiences may be different. My symptoms were the same each time—exactly as I described earlier at my workplace environment. Because I experience the panic attacks in the same way, I can identify when they are happening and start working on calming myself down with what I have learned and wellness practices to prevent them from escalating.

Other commonly known disorders that I have not experienced but know about:

- Separation anxiety disorder is usually associated with children separating from their parents.
- Social anxiety disorder makes individuals feel fearful of social situations because of feelings of embarrassment and self-consciousness.
- Specific phobias cause intense anxiety of a specific object or situation. I have met people with different kinds of phobias regarding snakes, frogs, roaches, and crossing bridges. I found the person with a bridge-crossing phobia (gephyrophobia) very interesting. He would find alternative routes to avoid bridges, as he feared the bridge could fall while driving on it. I must say that he was not afraid of flying on a plane but would not take a train ride if the route included a bridge.

I find this topic intriguing. Overall, we understand what anxiety is, when it is healthy, and when is not. We must have compassion for ourselves and not feel ashamed for seeking professional help or getting evaluated. Though we have made progress throughout recent years on the subject of mental disorders, we need to continue tackling one of the biggest reasons why people don't act on behalf of their mental health: the stigma associated with mental health issues. This stigma often comes from misconceptions and lack of information. Once we learn more about mental health and get rid of the negativity associated with it, we will all feel more comfortable talking about it and working on wellness.

Chapter 3

The Stigma

Before understanding that I had an anxiety disorder, I figured I was being insecure, overly worried, sensitive, or had a weak personality. I also felt guilt from what I perceived as not just being content with what was good in my life. I considered myself to be rich just for having clean running water. There are many parts of the world that don't have access to it. Water is life—isn't that enough? The mixed emotions were a constant battle that went on for years in my mind. I kept myself busy as much as possible so I would not be alone with my thoughts. The more tired I would get by the end of the day, the less time I had to think. I was basically distracting myself to avoid dealing with my thoughts. The more productive I was, the better I felt. If I had accomplishments in my personal life and work, that meant I was okay, right? I had people that loved me, a steady job, an immaculate single-family home, and a car; I had served in the military, graduated from college, gotten married, and given birth to a beautiful daughter. Basically, I was living the American dream. The effort that I put into convincing myself that everything was okay was weighing me down and was very exhausting.

There were periods of time I wanted isolation, stress ate, felt body aches, had no energy, was not sleeping well at night, and doubted every aspect of myself. I felt inadequate no matter what

I did. I did not share my feelings with anyone. I was embarrassed and cried a lot in the shower, mainly because I did not understand why I was feeling the way I did, and I did not know how to fix it. I often wondered if I should be doing more with my life. Growing up, I always worked to achieve a goal or reach the next life milestone. Without having a goal or a way of being recognized, I felt disappointed with myself. Looking back, if I had sought out professional help in my early twenties, I would have learned how to manage my mental state better, sooner. The reason I did not ask for help was mental health stigmas.

The American Psychiatric Association provides classes of mental health stigmas from a review of studies showing that while the public may accept the medical or genetic nature of a mental health disorder and the need for treatment, many people still have a negative view of those with mental illness. Researchers identify different types of stigmas:

- **Public stigma** involves the negative or discriminatory attitudes that others have about mental illness.
- **Self-stigma** refers to the negative attitudes, including internalized shame, that people with mental illness have about their own condition.
- **Institutional stigma** is more systemic, involving policies of government and private organizations that intentionally or unintentionally limit opportunities for people with mental illness.

These stigmas are stopping individuals who need help from seeking it. We need to work on eliminating them by educating and becoming comfortable talking about mental health issues. To alleviate some of the misconceptions, I would like to address a few of these stigmas from my point of view:

If you seek help for mental issues, that means you are crazy.

If you are seeking help, that means that you are concerned and care enough about yourself to get a professional opinion, regardless of what sort of medical issue you are experiencing. If you are proactive, you see a doctor on yearly basis for an overall health screening that includes your mental health. Acting responsibly toward your body is taking care of it.

If you seek help for mental issues, you will get medicated.

Not everyone gets medication after going to the doctor. Psychotherapy (e.g., counseling) may be suggested. If you do need medication, I strongly suggest you see a psychiatrist, as that is their specialty. I personally benefit from both psychotherapy and medications. It may take some trial and error to determine what works best for you, but don't get discouraged. We are all unique, and you need to work with your specialist until you are satisfied with your treatment. To address this misconception further, if you go to any doctor for any reason and you feel the doctor is medicating you without giving you a proper screening, checkups, or tests, do not hesitate to obtain a second opinion from a different doctor.

You don't need help; just shake things off and be strong.

People who make comments like this are not in your shoes. Their intentions may be to lift you up, but instead they are diminishing your feelings. I do agree that we need to be strong in life. You need to learn coping mechanisms and have the right support system to develop and keep your mental strength. However, mental struggles can occur for various reasons and escalate quickly. They are not something that can be shaken off; they require medical attention.

You don't need mental help; you just need to have faith and pray.

I will never underestimate the power of praying, because I have seen it work in many situations. However, here is my advice: have faith, pray, and seek medical attention. I don't understand why you would need to pick and choose from the resources available when they all help in different ways.

Once you have a mental issue, you will always have a mental issue.

Learning how to manage your anxiety in time can prevent it from getting worse. Sometimes people have situational anxiety or depression that can be treated for a short while, and treatment can stop once the person's symptoms improve. An example of this is dealing with the death of a loved one or a job loss.

People with mental issues can't function in society.

This can be said for any medical issue that is not managed. No one can function well if they are in pain or have an untreated medical issue. But if the pain and issues are managed and properly cared for, people can be productive. Many people around us with mental issues hold a daily job and parent their kids effectively. I am proof of it, and I can name many others in my work environment, family, support groups, and neighborhood that can attest to this. In fact, most people that handle multiple functions in society are the ones who get burned out and develop stress and anxiety struggles because of the "all work, no rest" lifestyle.

People with mental struggles are dangerous.

This idea probably comes from movies or the media. Most people with mental struggles unfortunately struggle in silence. You won't even know they are struggling. I am not denying that some people could be unpredictable and dangerous even to themselves. Yet, this is why it's important to change the stigma to allow people to feel comfortable seeking help. If we can reach people early in their mental struggles, we can help them manage their issues and prevent it from worsening.

The Treatment Advocacy Center is a national nonprofit organization dedicated to eliminating barriers to the timely and effective treatment of severe mental illness. A published background paper titled "Risk Factors for Violence in Serious Mental Illness" summarizes the results of forty-five different research studies conducted in different countries, including the United States, and concluded with the following findings related specifically to mental illness and violence:

"Most individuals with serious mental illness are not dangerous.

Most acts of violence are committed by individuals who are not mentally ill.

Individuals with serious mental illness are victimized by violent acts more often than they commit violent acts.

No evidence suggests that people with serious mental illness receiving effective treatment are more dangerous than individuals in the general population."

You only develop mental issues if you experience trauma.

Mental issues can be developed from chemical imbalances in the brain, secondary to other medical issues or situational events and, yes, events that can result in trauma. Some mental issues can be short-term, while others may last longer. People who experienced trauma at any age are at a greater risk of developing an anxiety disorder that can occur right after the trauma episode or at any point after in their lives. I get mixed reactions from people when I state that I have been diagnosed with PTSD. Some expect me to tell them military stories about being on the ground getting shot at and are surprised to hear that I served on a ship, in the ocean, "away" from the boots-on-the-ground conflict. I will not digress from the main subject, but I will quickly clarify that the conflict not only exists on the ground and many military members possessing jobs in "safer" zones still encounter trauma. It is the nature of the mission and the environment.

Mental disorders are not visible in people, nor can we weigh situations or trauma types to determine whether someone should have a "right" to develop a mental disorder. We are all unique; you can have several people experiencing the same traumatic event, and you can see them each handle it differently emotionally. If you experienced a traumatic event and need to speak about it, seek counseling, regardless of when the event happened.

It's not postpartum depression; you are just tired, emotional, and a new mom.

I do not even know why there is a stigma in this area to begin with. A female body produces a baby, and there are numerous changes associated with that. If anything, we fail to recognize that the woman is having depression because we think it is all part of the experience. I was reminded that women have had babies since the beginning of time without any assistance and they were fine. Where they? And if this is proven, how would knowing this fact help me feel any better? The bottom line is, we need to support women who experience postpartum depression and not make them feel less of a mother or a woman because of it.

I was in my twenties and three months along when I accepted that I was pregnant. I was in denial at first because I did not have any symptoms—no morning sickness except for extreme constipation. Throughout the pregnancy I cried a lot, and I was very emotional, which was a consequence of hormones, I was told. I did not know much about babies. I was the only child, never babysat, and when I went to stores, I was intimidated by toddlers crying or screaming. Realizing that I would be someone's mother made me collapse to the floor in tears once. I wanted to be a good mother; I had fears of not being adequate. I studied motherhood as much as I could and took birthing classes at the local hospital. When I had my daughter, all my fears regarding inadequacy disappeared. I knew how to take care of my daughter; I was her mother and felt it. The delivery of my daughter was complicated, and we were in the hospital for two weeks. I did not tell anyone, but I feared that with all the people around us—the doctors, different nurses every four hours, friends, and even the military chaplain—that one of them could take my baby away. This is the first time I learned about postpartum depression.

In an effort to calm my thoughts and my suspicions of postpartum depression symptoms, I expressed my fears to the doctor when he asked me how I was adjusting to motherhood. His response was very clinical and not comforting at all: "If you don't get better in four weeks, we will have to medicate you for postpartum depression," the doctor said. "No way," I thought. I would not take medication, especially because I was breastfeeding my daughter, and anything I took would be passed to her. I was not depressed; I was just overwhelmed, I told myself over and over. I equated being fearful and overwhelmed with failing as a mother. I could discern that my fears were unfounded, but I could not control them. The weeks that followed were tough emotionally, but I had support around me and my wonderful baby. People were understanding of my emotions because they are justified by the experience of pregnancy. As time went by, the fears of someone taking my baby away faded. As a bonus, being a mother helped me take off the pressure I placed on myself to be put together all the time because I was now caring for another being, a being that reminded me how we are born with joy, simplicity, and love.

People who are depressed are suicidal.

Being depressed is not the same thing as being suicidal. Depression affects moods and overall daily performance. The American Foundation for Suicide Prevention reports "while the presence of a mental health condition may contribute to increased suicide risk, it is important to note that the majority of people who live with mental health conditions will not die by suicide."

Suicidal thoughts, on the other hand, take people to a place of hopelessness and desperation. Suicide may appear as a solution to stop the mind, the feelings, or a quick "fix" to a problem. However, this is an erroneous thinking or state of mind that doesn't take into consideration the fact that appropriate treatments help, solutions to problems do exist, and circumstances change, as nothing lasts forever. Patience is required. Depression can lead to suicidal thoughts if untreated. It is very important that you know there is always hope. If you are having suicidal thoughts, get help immediately, don't be alone, and stay in a safe environment until help arrives. Once you are at a better place emotionally, start working on a plan to change your situation, build a support system, and follow the recommendations of a mental professional.

Life is a constant Ferris wheel ride. It goes up and down, and sometimes you like the ride, but sometimes you feel like throwing up. When you are at the top, you can see the big picture. When at the bottom, you don't see much at all, but you know it will go up eventually; it is just a matter of patience and the understanding of how it works. Now, if the Ferris wheel does not go up at all or has trouble performing, repair is necessary. Once repaired, the Ferris wheel will move as intended once again.

Chapter 4

The Unthinkable

As a teenager, my romantic relationships were very intense, passionate, and, to an extent, unrealistic. My level of immaturity, insecurity, and need to be accepted led me to put myself into premature adult situations while still being a child. I do not know if it was the telenovelas, the hormones, past negative experiences, or something in the air that made me crave codependent relationships. There was a particularly toxic relationship in my life; even though I knew it was clearly not good for me, I could not stay away from it because I was madly in love. So, when I heard of a girl in high school being hospitalized after taking a bottle of pills as the result of her boyfriend breaking up with her, I understood. I empathized because I, too, had considered this option a year earlier. Cheated on, humiliated, disappointed, and heartbroken—while holding a bottle of pills in my hands—I thought, "He would cry for me for a few months and move on." That thought made me stop and feel stupid. Deep down I knew my thoughts were wrong; I felt guilty for having these thoughts, and the depression settled in. I lost weight, dyed my hair blond, and wore blue contact lenses. While everyone saw my great-looking physical transformation, I was crying on the inside.

I did not share this experience with anyone because I was ashamed and in denial, thinking it was not a big deal. Typical teenage drama behavior, I thought. Back then, the risk factors and warnings of suicide were not a topic discussed in schools, churches, or at family dinner tables. All I remember is being a depressed, heartbroken teenager looking for a different direction in life. I wanted a fresh start somewhere new, and with only thirteen dollars in my bank account, the US Navy seemed like the perfect path to get going on a new direction.

The summer of the year 2000, I found myself sitting on a bus on the way to Naval Station Great Lakes, Illinois, for basic training with a lot of strangers. It seemed surreal. I do not know what was on the other people's minds, but as soon as all the recruits got off the bus, I could tell some were already regretting it. Not me—I was all in. The next three weeks were a challenge because my English was not good. I could somewhat understand, but I could barely put sentences together. Luckily, there is hardly any speaking during basic training. Halfway through training, one of my bunkmates took a bottle of pills and was taken to the hospital in pain. I recognized in hindsight that this individual had visible stress and experienced anxiety, but we were going through military boot camp—a place where you go to get tough, and weakness is not to be shown. I heard this person recovered, was discharged from the Navy, and returned home.

During my time in the military, there were many incidents of people experiencing high levels of stress, anxiety, depression, and suicide attempts. I am not going to address those experiences because there are many variables, work environments, and situations specific to the military and veteran population that would require information outside of the scope and purpose of this book, and that is not my intent. I am proud to have served in the military and understand that what I experienced, good and bad, while serving was part of the job description, whether I knew it or not. I am a stronger, better person, a survivor, because of the level of life exposure I experienced in the military.

After completing six years in the military, I decided to go to college since employers could not see past my high school diploma (never mind the years in military service). I was in a classroom with around twenty-five people, and it was the same group each semester. We all worked during the day and studied at night, pursuing a college degree that would guarantee better positions, opportunities, and pay. One of my classmates was a young individual who smiled a lot, kept good grades, and was very enthusiastic. On a random Monday, our class was informed that this individual had shot himself with a gun over the weekend and left a note to his parents. While people were talking about this event in the classroom, I did not know how to process the news. No one saw this coming. This individual did not give any indication that something was wrong at all—no warnings, no red flags, nothing . . . nada. I don't recall getting any emotional support about this from the school, and classes continued as usual since we were on a tight schedule to graduate in 2013. It was never revealed what could have been the reason for this individual to end life. It is hard to tell what people are going through, which is why communication, compassion and mental health awareness are important.

I have been managing anxiety, cycles of depression, and PTSD for a long time, and I am open about it. In December of 2019, a family member noticed when I took a prescribed medication during a family gathering and asked me about it. When I mentioned it was for anxiety, this family member was surprised because I looked well composed. Two months later, I received a book about meditation in the mail with a note of encouragement from this family member, asking me to give meditation a try as another way to manage anxiety. The book, a story about a reporter who suffers a panic attack on live national television and his journey to overcome anxiety, was *10% Happier* by Dan Harper. Meditation seemed key to his success. After reading the book, I followed the basic meditation practices every day as Harper described. It took a few months, but I finally learned how to slow down the mind.

Early in 2021, this family member notified me that he was also dealing with anxiety and depression. He'd experienced a panic attack and been hospitalized. I was not able to visit since we lived in different states, but we shared a few phone conversations regarding experiences, medications, wellness retreats, and other mental health topics. This family member was being treated and continued to look for wellness strategies. However, when I received the news mid-year that this person had committed suicide, I could not believe it. Deep sadness rushed in fast.

Once again, I found myself not knowing how to process the news. My first thought was, "No, wait! I have so much more to share on how I manage my mental state that maybe could help you, too." Sadly, I was not able to share much of it, and I still wish I could have.

When someone is overwhelmed, it is hard to convey everything you want to say at once, so I wanted to gradually continue to converse and provide support to this family member as I had the chance. I really thought this family member was going to be a recovery success story, because this individual was looking for answers and ways to get better. I later found out more about this situation, but out of respect for the family's privacy and since the loss is still recent, I will refrain from discussing more details.

This family loss triggered in me another cycle of depression that lasted a few weeks. I kept asking myself, If I can manage my mental health, how can I help others do the same? The way this family member described feelings and symptoms sounded familiar to me because I had felt the same way at some point. My inner reflection on this sad situation woke up a desire in me to do something about it, to give hope and help others somehow. I also kept wishing I could have conveyed everything I knew regarding how I manage my mental state to see if something, anything, would have helped this family member with his situation. I started to write as a way of healing. Writing for myself did not feel motivating, but I had to get stuff off of my chest. This is when the idea of writing a book in hopes of helping other people struggling set in. I cared, I wrote, and I cried a lot, but I kept writing.

Our lives have value, and we are all equally important. We all deserve a beautiful, happy life. Regardless of where we are, or what we are experiencing, there is always hope. It only takes a small speck of light to penetrate even the darkest room. Don't ever give up on life.

Important note! If you or someone you know are experiencing suicidal thoughts, contact the National Suicide Prevention Lifeline or dial 911 immediately. If you are not in the United States, call your local police or medical emergency department.

The American Foundation for Suicide Prevention advises the following steps if you suspect someone is at risk of suicide:

1. Have an honest conversation.
2. Talk to them in private.
3. Listen to their story.
4. Tell them you care about them.
5. Ask directly if they are thinking about suicide.
6. Encourage them to seek treatment or contact their doctor or therapist.
7. Avoid debating the value of life, minimizing their problems, or giving advice.

Chapter 5

Spirituality and Inner Work

There are many rhetorical questions regarding our purpose on Earth and why we exist. These questions are important because they make us look inside ourselves for a deeper meaning in a way that our five senses can't explore. Are we living a meaningful life? We are susceptible to good and bad experiences, and our beliefs will play the biggest role on how we feel and respond. Whether we are surrounded by people or alone, our metal struggles are internal battles we need to face as individuals. You can have all the help in the world at your fingertips, but if you don't believe in yourself and a purpose higher than the physical shapes and our daily routines, your battle will be much harder to fight.

Knowing yourself and seeking spiritual development will help you withstand the hardships we experience in life. Strengthening your spiritual muscle will carry you when you need it the most. Treat spirituality like any muscle in your body—you need to exercise to make it useful and strong. Everyone needs to work on their spirituality, especially people with mental issues, because this is the muscle ready to assist when negative thoughts and emotions arise. You can try to fight internally without any belief, tough it out, and somewhat succeed, but that has not been my experience. As Franklin D. Roosevelt said, *"Physical strength can never permanently withstand the impact of spiritual force."*

I can weather the storms in life by having faith that things are going to be okay. It's remarkable to witness people dealing with tragedies in a graceful way. They do so because their faith is greater than the fear and the pain. They know pain is temporary. When I witness this strength in others, I empathize with their situation and believe that I, too, can have this strength. Our emotions are powerful, but we need to process and express them in a constructive, healthy way. This is easier said than done, but the truth is that our emotions don't change situations. Emotions help us or break us. It is up to us to be the manager of them.

I don't like to judge; I do question people's actions at times out of curiosity or confusion. If you are spiritually strong, a skeptic, or somewhere in between, we can all agree that learning is an everyday process. Our experiences and circumstances have shaped us in one way or another, but we still have the free will to decide what to believe. Our actions should be consistent with our beliefs and values. When dealing with mental struggles, looking at ways to explore deeper meaning in life is worth discussing.

Religion. I was advised to stay impartial toward religion for the purpose of this book, but I can't deny that faith has been an important healing aspect in my life. I do not have all the answers, but I can tell you that faith has aided my mental struggles. I have been a Christian all my life and I believe there is one God who sacrificed his son for humanity. I live by faith, not by luck, chance, or fear. Having this belief gives me comfort in the face of adversity. I am still human and have made both mistakes and excellent choices in life. I am not as advanced in faith as I would like, which is why I attend Bible studies in addition to Sunday service. I like to learn in a group setting because to be honest, I need the accountability to stay engaged. Being part of my church community makes me feel comfortable and supported. When I'm feeling anxious or need someone to talk to, there has always been someone to give me words of encouragement and pray for me. In times of depression or isolation, someone has reached out to see how I am doing. Finding a church while in the military was not easy. By the time I found a good one, it was time to move again to our next duty station. Once I got out of the military and established myself in one place, I researched and attended a few churches until I found the one that best aligned with my values. If you want a relationship with God, decide right now. Evaluate where you are spiritually and value yourself enough to work on your spiritual growth. There is a greater power that loves you, and there is more to life than what you see.

Meditation. The goal of mediation, for me, was to quiet down the mind in order to calm the anxiety. This was an effort to get centered and connect with myself. I was introduced to meditation when I was practicing karate as a child. This practice helps us connect with oneself and be grounded. However, I'd forgotten all about it as an adult. Life just got busier, and so did my mind. As I mentioned on the previous chapter, a book I received as a gift from a family member motivated me to start meditating again. I placed a rug in my bedroom with some pillows, put on some soft meditation music, and sat down with my legs crossed and eyes closed. The first few weeks, my mind was all over the place and my legs were falling asleep. On the bright side, I came up with the best to-do lists during those times. Since meditating was not working, I spent five months trying to concentrate on my breathing, imagining walks on the beach, or repeating the mantra of "inner peace." I also tried guided meditation, but some of the voices were so soothing that I would fall as sleep right away. I was getting better every time but not able to completely clear my mind. Then one day after work, I was very tired mentally. My body was okay, but I felt drained emotionally. As soon as I got home, I sat down on my meditation corner and decided to take one big breath. I felt relaxed, so I stayed sitting a few minutes more. When I opened my eyes and looked at the clock, nine minutes had passed. Remarkably, that day was the first day I was able to meditate effectively.

The nine-minute meditation felt like a win until I recently learned transcendental meditation (TM) at a retreat. TM is so much easier than any other technique I have attempted. It is so simple, there is no way to mess it up and requires no effort. I am not a certified TM instructor, so I will not rob you from the experience of learning it correctly if you choose to try it. The TM technique is taught in the US by Maharishi Foundation USA, a federally recognized nonprofit 501(c)(3) educational organization. The organization defines TM as "a simple, natural, effortless technique practiced twenty minutes twice each day while sitting comfortably with the eyes closed. The TM technique allows your active mind to easily settle inward, through quieter levels of thought, until you experience the most silent and peaceful level of your own awareness—pure consciousness."

TM is part of my daily routine. I sleep better and feel calmer because of this practice. I noticed that I interrupt less when people talk because I am not anticipating what they are going to say. Overall, TM has helped me stay more in the present moment and keeps my anxiety in check.

Your Five Senses. Stimulating the five senses was advice I received from my psychologist. Using the sense of sight, hearing, smell, taste, and touch to calm anxiety is an ability we always have available and is free. Practicing connecting to your body, senses, and surroundings will help know what works best for you. This will be useful when you find yourself in a situation where you need to feel calm. I consider the ability to use our senses to calm the mind superpowers. They assist with staying in the present moment. When anxiety takes you to the future with the possible scenarios that can occur or the past to remind you how bad something went, use your senses to bring you back to the present moment. Ask yourself these questions: What are you sensing this moment? Can you describe it? How does it make you feel? At the airport recently, feeling anxious around a lot of people, I asked myself these questions. The sense of smell was the predominant sense because of the nearby aroma of strong coffee. I could smell that it was sweet; I could detect cinnamon combined with a nut flavor of some kind. It made me crave a pumpkin spice latte, which I associate with the holidays and the remedy for cold weather. The smell-analyzing exercise, asking these three questions, took my mind away from the anxiety of being in the airport surrounded by a rush of people.

Journaling. Writing can be very healing, inspiring, creative, and relaxing. Writing your feelings down may be easier than speaking them out loud. The idea of expressing thoughts on paper makes it more official since you take one of the many thoughts in your head to write down—but you selected it for a particular reason. Good journaling involves writing down everything that comes to mind. Doing so avoids staying superficial or trying to control what you are writing. Don't be surprised if you get emotional. Do not judge yourself for what you are thinking and keep writing. This was not easy for me, as I was worried that someone may find the journal. I also did not know what to write about. Writing about my feelings felt awkward, but I kept doing it until it was not. I had tried journaling before, but it never seemed to stick as a habit. Sometimes I wrote the dates but not always. I also found out that writing on the computer was easier for me than the journal. Here is my very first journal entry:

"I received this journal after spending over $50 at a bookstore. I want to write, to express but not sure where to start. I feel like getting this journal was a sign for me to start writing. This journal is so pretty. The pattern detail is in silver with gold flowers on a black background. It has a hard cover, looks fancy and priced at $15. I hope to continue writing, I don't have a strategy but will write what is on my mind in hopes to express and have some 'me' time."

There is really not a right or wrong way to journal; you just need to start writing until you find a writing flow that works for you, but you need to be honest with what you write. I inconsistently wrote for months. Sometimes I wrote pages, sometimes paragraphs, and sometimes I was too sleepy to write or did not feel like it. When I wrote, there were different types of feelings: optimism, hope, gratitude, happiness, planning, sadness, anger, disappointment, pity, and sometimes I cried. When I read this journal, I see how I evolved in expressing my emotions. I also see the repetitive issues that come up. Seeing themes lets me know what I need to pay attention to and work it out. If I am still feeling or writing the same thing for months, then there is some action needed, because that means I am clearly stuck. The following is a journal entry that I wrote while crying:

"I mean well but is seems that there is something I am not getting. I feel the sadness but no longer the pain. I never been the revenge type of person but feel disappointment at how some situations turned out. It is unfair. Where is my justice? There is depth in me, and I feel my emotions so purely. These emotions are a blessing and a curse."

When you express your feelings out through writing, they are exposed and no longer blocking you. In this journal entry, I was writing about a situation with a particular person I have not talked to in over a year. Clearly, this was something that still affected me. I had not written about this situation for a couple months, yet on this day it came up. This lets me know that I need to work on my feelings about it. Healing is all about accepting, processing, feeling the emotions, and letting go of what no longer serves us. You can connect better to yourself and others if you work on any emotional blockages you may have. The memories and lessons will always be with you, but you do have control over how you feel about it.

As an exercise, try journaling for a month. Write everything that comes to mind, even if what you are writing is all over the place and unrelated. After that month, read what you wrote every day. See if there are common themes. Do you feel the same way now? Have you seen changes in the way you feel or express what you feel? I have even felt embarrassed from some of the stuff I wrote because I was so over those feelings. I remind myself not to judge. The point of the exercise is to let the emotions out so we can work on them and heal.

I admire people who have taken trauma, adversity, and challenging situations and created something good out of it. They are public speakers, life coaches, founders of organizations supporting special causes, or writers who have the courage to publish their experiences. I have much admiration for these individuals and wish I could speak about all my experiences freely, without my voice cracking, feeling visibly uncomfortable, crying, or experiencing a panic attack. Writing has been easier for me than speaking. In a way, writing has given me a voice I did not know I had.

Traveling. While traveling away from all you know, from what is familiar to you, you pay attention to the present moment as you see what is new. Different scenery and ways of living open your eyes to uncertainty and changes. Why is this important? Because we are meant to grow, expand our horizons, and develop as people. You do not have to go to another country to experience this; you can drive an hour to a different town and your awareness will be stimulated instantly. This stimulation expands your curiosity and sense of adventure. It may also stimulate relaxation, as being out of your area means being out of your regular routine. When I traveled in the military, I always felt so small. I traveled to other countries, saw other cultures, and wondered about the many places in this world I had not seen. How amazing would it be to see the whole world? My second military deployment was on a ship. When I could, I would go out in the middle of the day and observe the ocean. We were surrounded by water with no land in sight. The ocean and sky meet at the distance, leaving no gap in between. One was light blue and peaceful; the other was dark blue and rough. Together they made the best relaxing scenery amid the stressful job I was there to perform. I remember staring into the distance, contemplating on the fact that we were so far away from everything, and we only had ourselves and the trust we placed on each other to survive. At that moment, I had no material things to worry about. Living on a ship was part survival and part unpredictability. The moments that I could be alone with the sky and the ocean made me reflect on who I was, the trajectory of my life, what really mattered, and where I wanted to go from there.

Wellness Retreats. Sometimes it's good to purposely get away and focus solely on yourself. Retreats often offer wellness education, healthy food, exercises, and activities intended to soothe the mind, body, and spirit. I specifically researched meditation retreats to get information for the family member I mentioned in earlier chapters who was dealing with anxiety and depression, but I also wanted to attend one myself. The ones I liked offered great programs ranging from three to ten days. Located in California and New York, the prices were excessively out of budget. I narrowed the search to local retreats and found a few farms offering quiet weekend stays for relaxation. I was considering one farm for its reasonable price and two-hour driving distance. It included a room, three healthy meals a day, quiet time in solitude, nature walks, morning yoga, and evening vegan cooking classes. However, the same week I was considering the farm weekend package, I received an email from the Warrior Progressive Alternative Training for Healing Heroes (PATHH) stating that I was accepted into their program, and six months later I was on my way to the Big Red Barn Retreat in South Carolina.

Warrior PATHH is a post-traumatic growth-based training program for combat veterans and first responders. The training consists of a seven-day on-site initiation followed by eighteen months of training delivered by instructors through a web-based platform. I described this program as an emotional boot camp: sixteen to eighteen hours a day of classroom exercises, outdoor activities, and learning specifically crafted for personal healing and growth. I broke down emotionally and self-reflected about my life in a way I had not done before. This happened because the program was effective. I had been working on myself for years, but I wouldn't have gotten as far as I did without the program and the wonderful staff, mainly because I was gently pushed and assisted while facing my internal self. I can't describe the healing I experienced alongside six other women who also attended the program. This was an experience that got me closer to the real me. I wish everyone could attend a program like Warrior PATHH. I have heard there are programs for the civilian population via different organizations; it is just a matter of researching what they are and the qualifications. Unfortunately, my family member did not qualify for PATHH because of the veteran or first responder requirement. He also took his life before I attended this program. I was not able to share this experience or what I learned. As painful and challenging as this growth experience has been, I have learned a great deal about myself and what kind of life I want to live. I want authenticity, peace, and personal fulfillment.

Volunteering. It feels good to assist other people, organizations, or a special event that involves a good cause, especially if it has a meaning or a connection to you. It also puts your own situation in perspective and causes you to reflect on whether you've taken your blessings for granted.

I have a heart for service to others, but I have found that I am not emotionally fit to volunteer for certain causes. Although I am working on my mental strength, some charities deal with heartbreaking scenarios that affect me emotionally. I need to protect my mental health by putting myself in suitable situations. For example, I volunteered at an animal shelter for six months until I noticed I was becoming depressed. The animals were so loving that I could not comprehend how anyone could neglect or abuse them to the point they had been. Prior to this experience, I volunteered one hour at a children's hospital where kids were being treated for terminal illnesses. I stayed one hour because I started to cry uncontrollably, and at that point, I was no help to anyone. In fact, the people working there had to console me. At work, I volunteered for events, donated blood, helped organize fundraisers, and collected toys and coats during the holidays for a homeless shelter. I like carrying out events to help, but I prefer to work directly with the people that need assistance.

Working full-time leaves little time to volunteer, so I must get creative. I have been volunteering at a food pantry for a couple of years. It has been a good fit for me because it has been less emotional than other volunteer opportunities. The volunteers in the group have become friends. Serving as a Spanish translator, I have gotten to know different people with different backgrounds and situations. I have been asked for hugs, received many smiles, and comforted some that needed to talk and cry. There is something special that happens inside of ourselves when we connect with and help one another.

"*What you have is momentary; who you are is forever.*" –Frank Sonnenberg. You are unique and perfect in your own way. If you fail to see your own value, then that should be your purpose at this moment. Start seeing yourself from a different perspective and work on finding out who you really are. This will require honest self-reflection, trying new things to explore your abilities, reading, and anything you can think of that would enrich you. Basically, you are performing a study, an exploration of yourself as you would with someone you are going to date because you want to get to know them. Decide you are worth it right now, because you are. You are not your circumstances, and your experiences were meant to teach you something of value. You are not in competition with anyone, nor must you prove anything to anyone other than yourself. There will be things that you can't change or control outside of you. As for the rest, you decide how to handle it. You have more power in your own life than you think.

Chapter 6

Emotional Support

Seeking comfort from others does not come naturally when struggling emotionally. We tend to hide or attempt to resolve our emotions ourselves. Sometimes, alone time can help clear the mind, but other times you need support from another human being. When I was in denial about my anxiety disorder, I was doing okay and even got used to the nervousness and negative thoughts. Negative thoughts are like tons of bugs in the air while you try to walk a beautiful path—you wave them away, but they are annoying and distracting. You can still walk through the buggy path, but you are doing it inconveniently. While dealing with the anxiety struggles, I did not reach out for help. Being a strong and put-together person was my image, my identity, and what I thought was expected of me. This identity I was holding on to was ironically what was breaking me internally. I was a fraud. I was okay on the outside, but on the inside, I felt insecure about my abilities and afraid of failing in life, whatever that meant. I was very sensitive during my depressive cycles and wanted to isolate, though I carried daily life like I always did, so no one had an idea I was even depressed. I would tell the people that noticed that I was tired, not feeling well, or had not been sleeping regularly. I was fooling others while also fooling myself.

Opening up to someone about what is going on in our heads is not easy, and it's awkward. You have options on who you can talk to, and you should talk. If we were meant to be alone in this world, we would be a glacier floating on our own course. If you feel comfortable talking to a loved one, that is a good start, but keep in mind that there are specialists trained to help you when you find it hard to cope with your emotions or situations. Sometimes, you just need someone to talk to. Other times, you may need to speak with a professional who can evaluate and provide you with a wellness path to move forward. Again, this does not necessarily mean medication. Also, you do not need to have a mental struggle to benefit from mental health counseling. Consider adding counseling to your wellness plan.

Family and Friends. You may have an understanding family who may have experienced what you are going through or are supportive even if they don't understand, and that is wonderful. Overall, family and friends love you and they mean well. However, sometimes the way they approach mental health comes across as dismissive or uncompassionate. Their reaction is out of fear or lack of understanding. Family and friends are typically the first group of people we may want to open to because they are around us. We may want an opinion on whether what we feel is normal or not. Unfortunately, they are not mental help professionals. In my experience, I received a lot of comments like "Everyone experiences hardship; you just have to be strong," "Pray about it," or—my favorite—"Other people have it way worse than you do." There is some truth to their comments, and they may be trying to give you tough love. Their view is another way to look at things, but this approach diminishes your feelings or whatever emotional turmoil you may be going through. You may end up feeling weak, guilty, or suppressing your feelings, especially around them. It is very important to communicate how you are feeling, but if the reaction you receive is not of understanding, then reach out to other support systems.

Spiritual Counselors. This category comes usually in the form of a mentor, religious leader, or someone more advanced spiritually than you are. Like any type of counselor, you need to research, ask for references, and so on. I found a counselor at church who provides a spiritual approach to mental health rather than the clinical approach. I meet with both my clinical psychologist and the spiritual counselor, who also happens to be a psychologist. In simpler words, her approach includes Bible references for dealing with life situations—in my case, with mental struggles. Always use discernment when you listen to others. If something does not feel right, find another counselor. It is very important you find a place that you feel comfortable, and their values and principles should align with you and the truth. No one has 100 percent of the answers, but in one way or another, deep down, we know and feel we are in existence from something other than flesh.

Mental Wellness Organizations and Local Community Resources. Community or city programs sometimes offer free yoga, recreational sports, and other activities to promote health. Although most of the programs concentrate on physical health, a portion of it also includes mental wellness. If you have health insurance, you can also call or search their website for mental wellness programs. Some offer rewards or discounts toward your premium. The idea of participating in these programs is to learn, improve your health, and connect to more resources available. You may research these programs or other information regarding mental health, anxiety, or stress reduction online, but never attempt to diagnose yourself. The best treatment will come from a health professional. As for any information you find online, make sure the resources are legit.

Animal therapy is a stress management technique that is becoming more popular. Animal therapy places provide a one-on-one session with animals. There are also several organizations that train animals to detect sudden fluctuations of emotions in people. These animals learn how to act in a way that relaxes the person they interact with. At the Warrior PATHH retreat, I had the opportunity to try equestrian therapy, and I loved every minute of it. I was able to make a connection with a horse, brush his hair, and walk him. For the horse to walk next to anyone, there has to be a connection established first. The minute you get distracted, the horse stops walking because you broke the connection, and they no longer have a direction or desire to follow you. Horses can sense your emotions and feed from them.

I am an animal lover and like to be around them. I have owned pets all my life, and they are such a joy. Pets bond with you no matter how you look or smell, what you say or do. They offer unconditional love. Interacting with animals is therapeutic. Animals live in the present, trust their instincts, and are authentic. Seeing them in their natural environment is relaxing. If you are not able to have pets, consider petsitting for someone else, volunteering, visiting a zoo, or simply taking a nature walk to see what you may come across. If you are exploring new territory, make sure to research the local animals in the area and follow safety precautions. I once saw a beautiful brown bear cub in the woods. I wanted to stop and take a picture, but someone reminded me that if the cub was in front of me, the mama bear was probably not too far. We left immediately. After seeing that cub in its natural environment, it is hard to see bears in the zoo—but that conversation is for another book.

Employee Assistance Programs (EAP), School Counselors, or Social Workers. These resources are usually free and confidential.

People have expressed being afraid even asking for information because it may affect or look bad on their employment or school record. There should not be negative consequences for participating in mental wellness programs, nor should it be used against you in any way. If you think you are being treated differently because of it, consult a legal adviser. There are employment positions that require favorable mental evaluations. In such cases, if you are determined not to be mentally capable of fulling those positions, do not take it personally. It is in your best interest and the best interest of others that you not be placed in a job position that may affect or aggravate you mentally. After all, the number one priority should be your health and safety.

I once considered applying as a 911 operator, but after reviewing the job requirements, I determined it would not be a good position for me. I am empathetic and emotional. If someone calls 911 screaming for help, I will probably start screaming and crying for them simultaneously during the phone call. This is probably a skill I could learn over time, but to protect my mental peace, I choose not to put myself in high-stress situations. Maybe one day I will be in a position to endure high levels of stress, but right now is not that moment.

Take time to learn about the benefits you have available at work or school. Don't wait until you have a panic attack to find out. I was referred to the EAP for assistance after an on-site panic attack. This event did not affect my evaluations or promotions. Some employees get time off or even short-term disability, if needed, for panic attacks. I was not given time off, but my employer made a few changes to my work environment that benefited all workers. I also received a referral from the EAP for sixteen paid counseling sessions at my nearest family counseling facility. I was reluctant to attend, but the sessions turned out to be beneficial. I learned so much about stress in the workplace that I became the wellness lead for my work site. With the assistance of Human Resources, I was able to organize volunteer events, a ten-minute paid chair message, and other activities to raise awareness regarding mental health.

Family Doctors, Physicians, or Health Practitioners. This group of professionals assess your overall health and provide immediate attention to anything related to your health. They are qualified to diagnosed anxiety and depression and may recommend psychotherapy, medication, or both. If you are suffering from panics attacks or have persistent anxiety that is affecting you daily, ask your doctor for a referral to a psychiatrist to be evaluated, especially if you require medication. Psychiatrists specialize in mental health, and you want to be assured you are prescribed the most appropriate medication by a doctor who specializes in mental health. This is not different from going to the doctor for a heart problem and asking for a referral to a cardiologist.

Psychologists, Counselors, and Therapists. I am grouping these three categories of mental health professionals together, as they can help you identify anxiety, depression, or other mental struggles to determine whether you may have behavioral or psychological disorders. These professionals are all licensed, but they have a different level of education and different approaches to mental health. In most cases, you do not need a referral to make an appointment. Contact your health insurance to find out what coverage you have and what is included. There are in-person sessions as well as online sessions for easy scheduling and convenience. If you do not have health insurance, research mental health nonprofit organizations and check with your employer or school administrator for free or discounted resources.

At first, I held back a lot because there were things I was not even admitting to myself or felt ashamed to discuss. For decades, there have been experiences I did my best to forget or even blocked them out. Suppressed emotions have a way of affecting you slowly from the inside in a way that is hardly noticeable. The problem is that not dealing with suppressed emotions makes them build up until a trigger makes them burst out. These emotions may appear at the wrong time and with intensity. I once had a panic attack in the middle of watching a movie. It was not the movie that caused the panic attack but what the movie reminded me of. I excused myself and hid in the bathroom at first, then I went outside and stay there until I calmed down. Once again, I choose to walk it off and not follow up on it. I regret not looking for help sooner. I continued to deny my inability to control my anxiety. It took many years from this episode and many others for me to decide to make an appointment. Part of the reason I did not seek help is that I did not want to start crying in front of a stranger, especially a specialist who, in my mind, would probably think I was just being pathetic and worrying about the wrong things when the world has real problems. I finally did because I wanted to get better. The first few sessions were awkward, but as I started getting more comfortable talking, things begin to change. I participated in awareness exercises, learned coping strategies, and saw positive results in managing my emotions. I felt better; my confidence went up, and I was not avoiding myself but embracing me.

Psychiatrists. The first time I saw psychiatrist intake forms, I silently freaked out. Seeing the title alone made me feel like I was surrendering my power or rights to the doctors and could possibly be hospitalized against my will. I also thought about how seeing a psychiatrist could be used against me in court, even though I've thankfully never been in court. Anxiety and the mental health stigma were playing my emotions and causing disarray in my head about just filling out this form. Some of the terms used to describe mental health are intimidating, and we don't want labels or associations with anything that could be perceived as something wrong. We can get sympathy for many medical issues, but not necessarily mental issues. We must remember the goal is to better our mental state, and that includes seeing the right doctors. There is absolutely no shame in that.

A psychiatrist is the doctor who specializes in the treatment of psychological and emotional problems. To be honest, I did not know the difference between a psychologist and a psychiatrist. I thought that maybe the psychiatrist was the doctor you go to when you have completely lost it and no other doctor can help you at that point. Once I learned that the psychiatrist evaluates all aspects of your mental health and has the education and credentials to prescribe medication, I felt more comfortable seeing one. The medical approach may be through prescribing medication, psychotherapy, or both. Unfortunately, to schedule an appointment, you will likely need a referral as part of an intake process that could take some time. This may be an issue if you require immediate treatment; however, a family doctor, physician, or health practitioner is able to diagnose and prescribe psychotherapy or medication until you are able to receive an evaluation by a psychiatrist.

We do not have to face anything alone. Create a support system that works for you. Some people are private and tend to isolate. That is okay, but reach out to someone when the emotions become overwhelming. Even if you are particular and selective, create at least a two-person support team and add more as you feel comfortable or as is recommended. The first person is someone in your life you can trust personally, and the second person is a health professional. Having an emotional support system helps you express what is in your mind, receive another person's perspective, and find solutions or treatment, if needed, in a timely manner.

Chapter 7

Medication

I do not advocate for medication unless other wellness methods have been attempted first or it has been determined necessary by a mental health professional. If you experience a situation that causes anxiety, or even depression, you may be able to manage it by processing the emotions of what is happening, talking about it, and using relaxation techniques. Whatever you are going through, remember to reach out to your support system. Again, you don't have to go through anything alone. If you do not know where to start or are experiencing overwhelming physical or mental symptoms, you need to consult a medical professional as soon as possible.

I also do not advocate for self-medication of any kind. You may think that drinking may numb the pain, but not only will it not make you feel better after, but it could worsen the anxiety or depression. The same goes with any type of drugs—legal, illegal, your aunt's pills, or any other idea you may want to try because you are hesitating to seek help or think what you are going through is not a big deal. You are also running the risk of interfering with medications you may be taking for other conditions when you self-medicate. Let me remind you that your health is always a big deal, and there is no shame in seeking assistance. Also, beware of herbal products, dietary supplements, special teas, or anything claiming to reduce anxiety, as most of these products are not monitored by the Food and Drug Administration (FDA) for a determination of risk and benefits.

If you search on the internet for anxiety remedies, you will find all kinds of information that may or may not be correct. The best way to deal with anxiety symptoms that are difficult to control is seeking medical professional assistance. There are many treatment options you can explore with your health professional. They may suggest individual therapy for a specific period and follow-ups as needed. Depending on your specific situation, group therapy may be another option. Sometimes it is easier to talk to people who can relate to what you are going through. There are other forms of therapy different from the traditional patient-doctor setting, such as art, music, or animal-supported therapy. The types of nontraditional therapy will depend on what is available in your area and what you feel comfortable with. Whatever plan you follow should be the plan you create with your selected professional.

If your symptoms require medication, have a proper mental evaluation with a psychiatrist. You may be paired with a psychologist who works under the supervision of a psychiatrist, but they do not prescribe medication; the psychiatrist will. Often, medication is prescribed in combination with psychotherapy. There are some medications for short-term relief, while others are prescribed for longer periods of time. It is important to always pay attention to your body and mind to note what you are experiencing. Benefits or side effects, no matter how insignificant they may seem, will help determine if the medication is a right fit or not. If the side effects are strong or your condition worsens, call your medical professional immediately. We tend to not read the side effects pages given at the pharmacy for a few reasons:

1. There are too many ingredients listed that we can't even pronounce.
2. You never get side effects, so you don't think you will get any.
3. You trust the doctor and that is good enough for you.
4. You are afraid that after reading the side effects, you won't take the medication.

I get it. I was afraid to take medication because I thought I would become slow, not myself, or be dependent on it. To avoid getting prescribed, I lied by saying I was okay when I was not. I guess I was not a very good liar, because the psychiatrist still prescribed me a medication for anxiety. What I was saying did not match my body language nor my answers on the evaluations. I was going to therapy occasionally but avoiding taking medication. I was mostly lying to myself, but the truth got exposed clearly when I experienced the very visible panic attack at work (described in chapter 2) and I was not able to control it. After that incident, I started taking the medication as I should have, because the reality of my mental health situation became undeniable.

When I started taking medication, I lost appetite in the beginning but was sleeping better. I made sure to annotate on my daily calendar any behavioral or physical changes I experienced to share with my doctor during the next visit. I was lucky to have the first medication prescribed work well for me. The medication dose was low, and after three weeks, I felt more relaxed, and my days felt less overwhelming. People noticed I was calmer when I talked and looked less stiff overall. I am not sure if the stiff comment was a compliment, but I felt periods of calmness without too much effort.

Your mental professional will prescribe a medication that best matches your symptoms and medical history. There are numerous medications available, and sometimes you may need to try more than one under the direction of your doctor until you find the one that is best for you. For awareness, I want to mention the major categories of mental health medication as defined by the National Alliance on Mental Illness:

- Anti-Anxiety Medications: Work solely to reduce the emotional and physical symptoms of anxiety. These medicines work quickly and are very effective in the short-term.
- Antidepressants: Improve symptoms of depression by affecting the brain chemicals associated with emotion, such as serotonin, norepinephrine, and dopamine.
- Antipsychotics: Reduce or eliminate symptoms of psychosis (delusions and hallucinations) by affecting the brain chemical called dopamine.
- Mood Stabilizers: Commonly treat the mood swings associated with bipolar disorder.
- Generic Medications: Generic medications and brand-name medications are not the same. The FDA only requires that generic medications contain the same active chemicals as those in brand-name medications and that the route of administration (whether the medication is available as tablets, capsules, patches, or injections) be identical.

It should be noted there are other nontraditional treatments for cases that do not respond well to medication or psychotherapy. These treatments may involve electrical currents in the brain, deep brain stimulation, magnetic stimulation, and I am sure you will hear of more as science continues to discover new options every year. I won't go into detail on any of these treatments because I want you to start with the basics and consult your mental health professional for the treatment options that are most appropriate for you. It is important for you to be involved in your treatment and communicate truthfully about how you feel. This will save you time in finding what works and may prevent the symptoms from worsening. If your anxiety is caused by another medical issue or condition, make sure to address that condition, as it may alleviate your anxiety by association. For example, if you have thyroid problems, which has been linked to anxiety, make sure you work with your doctor on treating your thyroid, as this may get your anxiety under control. Keep all medical providers aware of your overall health and treatments.

If you are taking medications for other conditions, check if those medications have anxiety or depression as a side effect, because that could cause or aggravate your mental state. If that is the case, do not stop the medication but contact your doctor to discuss the possibility of a prescription switch to a medication that will still treat your medical condition without the adverse side effects. If you are taking medication specifically for anxiety and depression, be aware of inadvertently selecting over-the-counter medication that may interfere. Some supplements, cold syrups, and allergy medicines, to name a few examples, have warnings on the label advising you to ask your doctor if you are taking antidepressants. Make sure you read labels before you buy the product and most importantly, make sure to consult your doctor. Pharmacists may be able to assist with medication questions, but they do not have your medical history and haven't examined you, nor are they qualified to do so. For this reason, I will continue to say: always consult your doctor.

If you must take medication, always take it as instructed. It is imperative that when you take medication, you still take care of yourself in every other area of your life. Medication alone won't help your medical problems; you still need to take care of your body and mind. Create a healthy lifestyle to the best of your abilities, love yourself enough to do so, and continue to learn ways to improve your quality of life. Take care of yourself and your body, and live life intentionally.

Chapter 8

Healthy Lifestyle

Living a healthy lifestyle is imperative to mental health. As simple as this may sound, often we put our work, family, studies, or any other area in our lives first, and slowly, we neglect ourselves. You do the best you can to include healthy meals and go to the gym when you find the time. It is good that you put effort toward your health when you can, but what will really make changes stay is having the mindset of living in a healthy way.

There is a lot of information on nutrition, fitness, stress management, and the benefits of social interactions, but it is tricky to apply it. The truth is, you may have to come up with your own definition of a healthy lifestyle that fits your actual lifestyle. Why? Because there are too many variables from person to person, and it will be difficult to fit all of us on one checklist. The stage of life we are in also determines what is considered healthy for your body. It is healthy for a baby to sleep pretty much all day, but not for an adult. Yet, some people do require more sleep than others to function properly during the day. We should not be all put to the same standards. It is up to you to create your own. Yet, as the unique individuals we are, we still have a few things in common that we need to take care of:

Basic Needs. At a minimum, you need to take care of your personal hygiene. This is what we are taught as children: bathe and wash your hair, brush your teeth, apply lotion, etc. When dealing with depression, the very basics may seem daunting. You may not even want to get out bed. However, if you are in a state of depression, don't think of all the things you have to do for the day; just think about practicing basic hygiene. Doing so will help bring up your mood and you will be giving yourself some self-care.

Sleep. Make sure you are getting enough sleep to allow your body and mind to rest. You will have more energy and be less moody throughout the day. Sleep should be a priority, as it affects both your mental and physical health. If you are having problems falling or staying asleep, see a doctor.

Eat Well. We all know we need to include fruits, vegetables, whole grains, and all the good stuff in our diets. I don't particularly enjoy cooking, but I cook and like to eat home-cooked meals. I meal plan every week, pack my lunches to take to work, and freeze leftovers if there any. If I eat at a restaurant, I try to select the healthiest option. This does not mean ordering a salad, but in choosing between fried potatoes or baked potatoes, I will choose the one that provides the most nutritional value.

The Mayo Clinic organization recommends avoiding alcohol, smoking, and drinking caffeinated beverages, as they can worsen anxiety. I do not smoke but I consulted my doctor regarding having a glass of wine during holidays or special events and received the okay. You need to find out from your doctor what is acceptable on your case, especially if you are taking medication. I am very glad my doctor concurred with my daily coffee intake, as it is a nice treat in the mornings.

Breathe. This sounds primitive, but anxiety makes the body breathe faster or even hyperventilate. Breathing was the first, most important milestone in our lives at birth. Its value has been taken for granted. Breathing has been the best quick relaxation technique I have experienced. My chiropractor told me once I did not know how to breathe properly. To show me, he had me stand back against a wall with one hand on my chest and another on my abdomen. He challenged me to breathe using my diaphragm. Apparently, I could not do it right. I was taking big breaths, moving my shoulders, neck, and chest. Trying to get the breathing done correctly made me feel dizzy, confused, and unsure of what I was doing. I went home and watched different videos. With a lot of practice, I was able to take the type of big breaths that expanded my diaphragm in way that felt good and relaxing. Breathing this way makes a difference when I need to feel calm quickly.

Exercise. It goes without saying that exercise has many health benefits. Staying active helps reduce stress significantly. You do not have to join a gym; you can walk around your neighborhood and gradually add more physical activities as you can. I personally do not like exercising by myself. I prefer playing sports. Unfortunately, I have some medical conditions as the results of injuries that require me to stick with low-impact exercises. This was not easy to accept. When I could no longer perform at the same physical level I once did, I felt weak and old. This was one of the reasons for my anxiety and depression. I was an athlete, carried a six-year military term, and related being strong to physical fitness and demands. Nonetheless, finding ways to stay active and fit it into our busy schedule is important. Whatever gets you moving, make sure you do it. I joined a gym several times but only seemed to commit for two months. What seems to work for me is having an accountability partner. My friend and I exercise in the afternoons or evenings during spring and summer. We walk different paths nearby for forty-five minutes. We talk so much that most of the time, we end up walking for over an hour. When the weather gets cold outside in the fall or winter, I do some exercises at home.

Wellness Checks. Once a year you should get your vision, dental, and overall health assessment completed. Most health insurance plans cover preventive care. If you do not have health insurance, there are free clinics and health fairs conducted by nonprofits that can provide you with a quick assessment. You cannot determine what your health looks like by looking at the mirror. You may feel good physically, but what would your blood work say? Likewise, you may think certain negative thoughts are okay, but if they are constant, disturbing, and affecting your mood, what would a doctor say? Do not gamble your health. Get your yearly checkups scheduled and attend your appointments.

Practice Self-Love. Have compassion toward yourself. Look how far you have come from birth. Your emotions have purpose, and you should acknowledge and process them. This will prevent them from building up and creating mental blockages. Pay attention to your self-talk. You should think highly of yourself, and do not put yourself down. Learn who you are and what you like. Explore your potential. Love your physical body. No one's suit is perfect, but it allows us to move, express, create, and live!!! You would not be able to do anything without it. I can keep going on this subject, but the point is that you need to appreciate your body fully, as it is. Your heart beats for you every day. It is cheering for your existence; don't take it for granted.

Socialize. Building connections and bonds with other people is wonderful. We deal with people on a regular basis in different scenarios, so we may as well find some that we can call friends and socialize. Some of these connections can evolve over time, and you may even get to consider them like family. Meaningful connections will help reduce stress and improve wellness, as you are communicating, celebrating life milestones, and enduring hardships together. You will have people to share moments with and be there for one another when needed. If you are feeling lonely or are new in an area, attend activities or visit places of your liking where you can meet people with similar interests. You should also consider being the one to host events. Often, people want to socialize, but no one wants to plan it.

If you are anxious around groups of people, socializing does not have to be challenging. You can go to places you feel comfortable, like the library, a park, study groups with limited seats, or any place less frequented by the masses or places spacious enough where there is room to move around. The amount of people to socialize with does not depend on quantity but quality. If you only have three friends, then meet frequently, share interests, and keep the connection flowing. Try to do so in person. Connections are more personable when you are standing in front of another. I understand technology is the way to go for many things, but to be able to share a laugh with someone is more joyful in person than with a screen in between.

Avoid Toxic People. There are people that are complete opposites from us, and that is okay—we can still be friends. We are not going to change them but let them be. We may even learn a few things from them. However, there are people that are very negative, inconsistent, controlling, and manipulative who play the victim, make everything about themselves, deplete your generosity, and have many other red flags that we ignore because we want to be nice. These people are toxic and will cause you more anxiety and stress. Their company is not worth your time, health, and energy. They may even involve you in their problems. If these people are family members, I understand you may not want to completely cut them out of your life, but you need to set strong boundaries and stick to them. You have a life to live with your own set of problems; do not try to carry theirs too. A lot of times, their problems are caused by their own doing. If people say they are going to change, believe their actions, not their words. Let them show you they have changed before you can reconsider lowering some of the boundaries. If you don't have to interact with a toxic individual, don't. Take them out of your life like bad weeds before they spread all over your entire yard. You are not ruthless by weeding toxic people out; you are protecting your peace and mind.

Healthy concepts are sometimes commonsense and basic. The problem is we are busy, and we have low energy and sometimes little motivation. We find ourselves trapped in the same patterns over time until it becomes the normal. We forget that the roles we play in our lives to keep up with our obligations and standards should not negate our well-being. Ironically, creating and living a healthy lifestyle leads to a better standard of living, thus providing a better quality of life. Obligations are better managed in a healthy state. My grandmother always reminds me that even little by little, you can still go far. Just keep moving forward. Start by making small healthy changes, adjust as you go, and the results will follow.

Chapter 9

Literal Organization

Who can possibly function effectively while disorganized? Don't get me wrong—some people can produce even when everything around them seems chaotic. This is because different people have ways to process and create systems that work for them, even if they look messy. The space we physically live in, work in, and how we spend our time affects our minds. If you have no type of organization in your spaces and daily routine or you can't find things or time to get things done, you will experience stress. Add that stress to a busy, overcommitted schedule, incomplete tasks, and before you know it . . . you are overwhelmed trying to meet all your commitments day by day without time to catch up and breathe. Feeling overwhelmed or being in constant stress leads to anxiety. It is only a matter of time before you physically and emotionally burn out. Time does not wait for you, and organization does not happen by accident. Make the time to assess and organize your spaces to simplify your life. This action is an investment in your overall wellness.

Living Space. Your living space should be a space that makes you feel comfortable and peaceful, a place that can restore your energy and rest. It also must be functional to accommodate your daily activities and other events. However, there a few things you need to keep in mind when evaluating your space:

1. Having less stuff is more. If there one thing I have learned from moving nine times in twelve years, it is having physical items to maintain, clean, use, and repair takes time, energy, and house space—in my case, only to pack up and move again. I am not a minimalist but prefer to have less. The amount of stuff you have is your decision. Keep whatever you want, but have it organized and have a system to manage your inventory so you can find what you need when you need it. It has been proven that visual clutter contributes to stress and anxiety. Clutter happens when there is more stuff than the space can store or there is no discipline to store things back in their designated area. My favorite quote regarding the relationship between stuff and life comes from Joshua Becker, a minimalist influencer and best-selling author. He said it best: "Intentionally living with less results in a life of less debt, less stress, and less anxiety." Have the intent to live in a home or work in a place where you feel comfortable and productive with the stuff that you need and get rid of the items that you don't need anymore that are getting in your way.

2. Create a space is that inviting to you . . . not guests, friends, or any other people you may want to impress. Many people follow the standard living space as they see on television or magazines, but does that work for you? I do not own a coffee table. I dislike coffee tables very much. I endured many bruises and pain because of coffee tables throughout my life until I decided to get rid of it for good. If I invite someone for coffee, I will serve it on the dining table or meet with them at a coffee shop. This is what works for me. No more dancing around the coffee table to avoid low sharp corners. Why have things that don't contribute to your comfort in any way?

3. Create a space for relaxation just for you. Find a place you can sit with items you enjoy. The purpose of having a corner in your living space is to train your brain to relate that space with relaxation time. This space can be anywhere you like, but only use it to relax. My space consists of a small rug with a throw pillow in the corner of my bedroom. Relaxation for me is meditation or literature; even the pets know not to come nearby when I am in my corner. A small table stands by the rug containing books, pictures, a journal, and a plant. Whatever space you choose, stay clear from electronics unless is to play relaxing music. The goal is to spend time with yourself to breathe, relax, and recover.

Workspace. Just like your living spaces, your working space needs to be organized for efficiency. You will spend a great deal of your day working, so make it count. Maintain your desk ready for productivity. On your computer, do not save everything on the desktop to the point it develops chicken pox. Organize in folders, network drives, or the shared cloud storage used by your organization.

I must confess that I live by my calendar (unless I am on vacation). When I schedule meetings or personal reminders to call people back or do training, I write everything I need to know on the calendar event description. I used to do this on a paper calendar, but with so many calendar features available electronically, I made the switch, and there is no going back to paper.

I am an advocate for to-do lists. I list everything that needs to be done, no matter how big or small the task is, so it gets done. I don't group them; I just write them down. On a typical day, I decide what to get done based on priority. However, if I am low on energy, I set a goal to complete at least three tasks that day at my own pace. In such low-energy days, I appreciate organization the most. If you have repetitive tasks, see if you can create templates or automate a process for saving time, consistency, and efficiency.

Schedule Your Time. Time is more valuable than money. Money balances on your bank account go up and down, but time only passes. Because time is so precious, you need to manage it wisely. There was a time in my life when my calendar was filled to capacity. I thought that filling out my calendar was an efficient way to manage time. If I was not doing something, it felt like I was wasting time. I could not even sit to relax because I would feel anxious about all the stuff pending that I could be doing instead. I also RSVP'd for every event because I did not want to miss out or felt like saying no was rude. My way of taking care of myself was scheduling medical appointments when needed or a physical once a year. The time off was for cleaning and catching up. Deep down, the overbooked schedule made me feel capable and accomplished. I was on top of everything, but eventually . . . it would lead to burnouts. I was not disorganized, but I was trying to handle too much in the same twenty-four hours we all get. Everything is about balance, and I did not have any. A good schedule should have your commitments but also time for yourself and what matters to you. What do you enjoy doing? Is it catching up with a friend over coffee? Family game night? Going fishing or gardening for relaxation? Working on a hobby or learning something new? When scheduling your time, think about the importance of each event or task. Don't be afraid to say no. It is your life, your time—decide how to use it intentionally.

Money Management. Money is a source of stress for many people whether they have any mental issues or not. The key to fix this issue is to have control over the finances. If you are not organized with money, it will come and go before your eyes. This will cause you to feel worried about not having enough, and if you experience an emergency, anxiety will kick in hard. However, if you manage your finances, no matter what happens you will be able to relax a little knowing that you have the finances ready to cover emergencies. I personally struggled with money when I became independent. I was eighteen and thought that a monthly budget was a list of all the bills with amounts. Whatever little money I had left, I saved twenty dollars and spent the rest. When I wanted something new on credit, I thought that if I could pay the monthly payment, that meant I could afford it. I never really paid attention to the interest rate on the overall amount. I was under the impression that the term *"borrowing"* applied to asking for money from a friend or family member, which I never did. I did not consider getting a loan or a credit card as borrowing because that is what the banks were there for, right? That is how you build credit, right? In my mind, I was building credit for my future—not borrowing. As you can see, the understanding I had for finances was not a healthy one. To make matters worse, I went to a vocational school during my high school years and obtained an accounting clerk certificate at graduation. Based on what I learned, "building credit" was financially savvy as long as you kept a balance sheet. However, this is not the case for personal finances; we need to be careful with consumerism.

Luckily, life is the best teacher one can ever have. Getting by with what I had and a little money extra to spend and save worked until my situation changed. The military relocated me, with the same wage, to another state where the living cost was higher. Although I was approved by the military to live off-base with an allowance, the process took over thirty days. Meanwhile, I signed an apartment lease and gave the first month's rent and the security deposit in advance, which left me with thirty-nine dollars to my name until the next payday, which was one week away. The apartment was ready to move into in four days, but I moved out of the on-base housing that same day. This meant that I needed to find a place to stay for four days with less than forty dollars. I was new to the area and did not know people I could ask for a stay. I was too proud to ask my parents for money because that meant at the age of nineteen, I was failing as an adult. I chose to stay in my car; after all, it was only for a few days. "I can tough this out," I thought.

It was very cold and uncomfortable. I cried, I hated it, and I was scared. I was homeless during those four days, but I did not see it that way because I had signed an apartment lease and in a few days, I was going to get the keys. I showed up early to work so I could shower in the gym. I ordered at fast food restaurants' dollar menus. A one-dollar bean burrito or regular taco goes a long way. I parked at a hospital so I could use the bathroom if I needed to in the middle of the night. I was afraid of someone figuring out my situation; therefore, my moves were strategic. The only good thing going for me at that time was that I had plenty of clean underwear. This experience made me promise myself to never allow a situation like this to happen again. My money views changed completely.

What followed from that experience was a new appreciation and respect for money and the things I had taken for granted for so long—a roof, a bed, a washing machine, heat, and many other things. But the biggest realization I received while sleeping in the car came while reflecting on how I was living my life. How did I get to this point? For the next few months, I counted every penny, every expense, identifying needs and wants, understanding that a savings account is not the same as an emergency fund and a budget is not a list of bills. I developed a strong determination to learn finances, realistic personal finances. I could not work on long-term goals if my everyday finances were a mess. I studied and attempted many methods to discover what worked better for my situation.

I improved my finances greatly, but over a decade later I found myself in debt again. This time, I had a family, and we were living a lifestyle we could not sustain. I was able to stay in a car at nineteen, but I could not do that again, especially with a child.

This realization came after I kept changing the budget to fit every bill and expense, and I could not make it work unless I paid some with credit cards. I used credit because our salaries were no longer providing enough money. It was not enough because we were living beyond our means. In addition to the basic bills, there were two car payments, two credit cards, a loan, and a camper. This was a reason to be anxious, and I was not sleeping well at night. I bought several books, but one of them changed my financial views completely. The approach was so radical that it changed me. *The Total Money Makeover* by Dave Ramsey provides simple steps to financial freedom, and nothing is sugarcoated. I won't describe his strategies because that is his work, and you need to perform your own research to decide how you want to move forward with your finances. In my case, Dave Ramsey provided powerful messages—in ways that pissed me off. He pointed out that my financial stupidity was my own doing—true, but I did not want to hear that. I thought about calling his podcast once to talk about how society has set up a system in which you can't progress without debt and to become financially free you probably have to live off the grid. I did not call because I was afraid he would chew me up and spit me out live on-air. I felt like he was blaming the people rather than the system. As I kept following his program, my financial posture improved and as time passed, he turned out to be right. We paid everything off and saved for emergencies. Vacations in the camper were more enjoyable after having no debt, and we even upgraded to a bigger camper. We do have control over our own finances regardless of how the overall country's economy is performing. The key is to plan your finances intentionally.

Throughout all the financial research, it never occurred to me to find a financial planner. I wish I had; it may have saved me time. Most banks, employee benefits, schools, and nonprofit organizations offer free assistance on personal finances. Be aware of companies interested in selling you products rather than helping you with finances. Organizing your finances will give you peace of mind.

Life is hectic and time is valuable. Organize your time, your spaces, and your finances. These are areas you can actually control in life, and having them under control will help reduce stress and anxiety.

Chapter 10

Live Consciously

Waking up in the morning breathing the air is wonderful and signifies the gift of another day. From that point on, every choice should be intentional. Don't do things out of habit; do things because you have a reason to do them. Embrace the high and lows and see the lessons from every experience. We can't hold on to time, so we need to make the best with what we have and go from there. Be conscious of how you live your life and live it with purpose.

Live In the Present Moment. Observe, learn, and experience new things in real time. These three actions will help you gain wisdom that, in turn, expands your capacity to help yourself and others. The past contains older iterations of who we are, and we are not to go backward. Take the lessons and move on. The future iterations of who we will become depends on how you live the present moment. Make responsible decisions and don't put yourself in situations that will impact you negatively.

Forgive and Let Go. We all have done wrong or have been wronged by others at some point. Holding on to resentment, guilt, or any negative emotions involving situations from the past only hurts us. Don't wait for an acknowledgment and an apology, because it may or may not come. Don't wait for your justice to be served, because you may or may not see it. It is best to cut the loss and move on. You will feel better and lighter when you let go because you are not tying your recovery to someone else or a particular outcome. You control your recovery by deciding to forgive. If you need to apologize to someone, do so sincerely without expectations on how the apology will be received. If you need to forgive yourself, do so with love.

Acknowledge Your Emotions. We are not made from steel, so we have no choice but to accept our emotions as a human trait and process them in a healthy way. Have compassion toward yourself and know that you are capable of so much more than you give yourself credit for. I used to think being physically fit and not showing emotions was strength. I decided to redefine what strength means because this way of thinking was breaking me emotionally. My new definition is ageless, simple, and as follows: Strength is developing and practicing resilience, gaining wisdom, and choosing compassion. What is your definition?

Take Time to Relax. Learn what helps you relax and do so regularly. Do not wait until you are stressed out because by that point, you will be so tense that relaxation will not be as easy to achieve. Make relaxation part of your schedule as a self-maintenance activity. Also, take vacations!!! No wonder you are stressed. If you are not feeling well, take time off. Many people show up at work because they have important deliverables or don't want to use their time off to stay home and rest. Don't risk getting worse or getting your coworkers sick too.

Be Positive. There is always more than one way of looking at everything—choose to see the bright side. This is a great way to keep the anxiety in check. Why worry about something prematurely? Until something is proven otherwise, stick with a good outcome. Avoid thinking negatively, feeling insecure, or anything that would bring you down. If you are sad, for example, avoid sad movies that would feed that emotion; try watching a comedy movie instead.

Know Yourself and Your Worth. When you know who you are, you don't seek external validation from anything or anyone. This is extremely important to understand. I know this very well, as I have exhaustedly attempted to seek validation from other people who—no matter what I did or how I performed—never seemed to acknowledge my value. This affected my confidence and self-esteem. When I started looking within and trusting my own abilities, I started to feel happier. This led to better job opportunities with significantly higher pay and relationships that were reciprocal. This also led to the fall out with some people. In becoming my own, I had to leave behind everything that was hurting or holding me back, and that included people, places, jobs, and things (coffee tables).

I have asked people if they love themselves, and the ones hesitating to answer have expressed reasons all leading to not feeling good enough. They feel they are not where they would like to be in life or not attractive anymore. Maybe someone else put them down. Some measure their self-love from their level of success, and I can keep going on the list of answers I got. All negative answers and not true.

I used to think that self-love was a rhetorical question for the purpose of reflecting on oneself, not necessarily a question to answer. I have been insecure, but as I started falling in love with myself, my confidence went up as to even consider exploring areas where I have no experience. I understand that I am not perfect but capable. I know that I am enough. I am proud for the many times I stood up after failures and for the victories I genuinely achieved.

I started seeing my own beauty once I stopped judging my imperfections. Your answer to whether you love yourself should be a resounding YES! The love for yourself should be unconditional. This means to love without the conditions of looks, job title, bank balance, and other people's opinions, situations, or circumstances attached to that love. You would not put conditions on your loved ones that way, so why would you do that to yourself? If you are not sure if you love yourself or if you know you don't, reflect on the reason why. Be aware of unrealistic ideas and talk it out with people who can help. You are your longest relationship. Love you!

Learn and Try New Things. Keeping your brain exercising by learning and experiencing new things is good for your mind and soul. Again, we did not come to Earth to pay bills and look pretty. We are growing and evolving beings. It is only natural to explore and be curious. I always learn something about myself when I try something new. I purposely look for activities outside my comfort zone. To mention a few examples, I entered a public library drawing contest, took an auditing job with zero experience, and went caroling knowing that my singing is not good. I also love learning and signing up for classes offered in my community, at a private institution, or online any chance I can. The classes that I have taken include cooking, cake decorating, nutrition, finances, home organization, French, hair braiding, yoga, painting, gift wrapping, modeling, wilderness survival, sociology, dog grooming, and many others. Knowledge is power, and I encourage you to keep empowering yourself.

Have Goals. Creating goals helps put our attention on what needs to get done to accomplish them. At the same time, we have something to work on and look forward to. When you aim at nothing, you are passing time, not to mention it is hard to feel motivated if there is no target to hit. Your goals should be realistic and help you advance in some way or at least give you satisfaction. Goals are not stationary; they will change as you go. When you reach a goal, create the next. The point is not to be always chasing something but to grow and continue building the best version yourself.

Volunteer. HelpGuide, an independent nonprofit that provides free mental health education and support, reports "by measuring hormones and brain activity, researchers have discovered that being helpful to others delivers immense pleasure. Volunteering helps counteract the effects of stress, anger, and anxiety. The social contact aspect of helping and working with others can have a profound effect on your overall psychological well-being. Nothing relieves stress better than a meaningful connection to another person."

It has been proven that helping others or a cause that aligns with our beliefs stimulates our overall happiness. You do not have to make an ongoing commitment; it may just be a matter of identifying who needs help nearby and helping them. If you are not used to helping others, practice will get you feeling more comfortable. In addition to helping people, communities, and the world, volunteering helps put life in perspective, as I mentioned in chapter 5. We are part of a bigger ecosystem. If we stay in our own nucleus, it is hard to connect and evolve. Volunteer opportunities have become more accessible with technology. You can now volunteer from the comfort of your home by coordinating events or pet adoptions, answering calls from domestic violence victims, and many other options. If you prefer to volunteer in person, there are many organizations that need the hands-on help. If you don't volunteer, that is okay too; volunteering does not determine if you are a good or a bad person. However, regarding mental health, volunteering does have many benefits that can help you while you are helping others. It is a win-win situation for everyone involved.

Educate and Raise Awareness. You don't have to go out of your way and start a mental health campaign—unless you want to. You could assist the people you know if they are willing to listen. As you learn about anxiety, you will notice it in other people easily. Sharing your experience may help other people relate to their experience and start the mental wellness conversation. I have been able to refer people to the right resources because they felt comfortable talking after hearing what I had to say. If people reach out to you for understanding, remember to always approach from a place of compassion. Be supportive and encourage them to seek the appropriate mental health professional.

When you live consciously, you are more in control of your emotions and outcomes. Live a balanced life and love yourself. Your entire body and mind need care, and if you need assistance, there is a specialist for every body part. Don't wait until your body breaks down or feels ill to seek medical help. Do it now as a preventive measure.

Anxiety or any kind of emotion won't stop you from living, but you need to manage them well, because the quality of your life will depend on it. Eliminate the stigma associated with mental struggles, promote a healthy lifestyle, and live the best life you can create. You owe yourself a beautiful life, and having anxiety won't stop you from accomplishing it. All you need is to learn how to make peace with it.

Acknowledgments

This book would not have been possible without the Self-Publishing School (SPS) Program and its wonderful staff. I had the vision to publish a book but had no clue where to start or how to do it. SPS taught me the process. I felt supported and became part of a great community of authors. Thank you, SPS, for providing the road map to follow on this journey.

I thank my daughter for her support and celebrating every book milestone with me.

I thank the readers for making it to the end. I wanted the opportunity of your time to read me out.

I thank God for always providing the path.

A Kindly Ask

If you liked my book, I kindly ask that you consider providing supportive feedback. Please, leave a review on Amazon or wherever you purchased this book.

I sincerely appreciate your time!

Sources

1. *Anxiety disorders.* (2018, May 4). Mayo Clinic Organization. https://www.mayoclinic.org

2. *Anxiety Disorders.* (2017, December 1). National Alliance on Mental Illness. https://www.nami.org

3. Dan Harris. (2019). *10% Happier: How I Tamed the Voice in My Head, Reduced Stress Without Losing My Edge, and Found Self-Help That Actually Works—A True Story.* Revised HarperCollins.

4. Dave Ramsey. (2013). The Total Money Makeover: Classic: A Proven Plan for Financial Fitness. Thomas Nelson.

5. Maharishi Foundation USA. (n.d.). What is TM? https://www.tm.org/transcendental-meditation.

6. *Stigma, Prejudice and Discrimination Against People with Mental Illness.* (n.d.). American Psychiatric Association. https://www.psychiatry.org/patients-families/stigma-and-discrimination.

7. Treatment Advocacy Center. (2016, June). Risk Factors for Violence in Serious Mental Illness. https://www.treatmentadvocacycenter.org

8. *Volunteering and its Surprising Benefits.* (n.d.). HelpGuide. https://www.helpguide.org

9. *What is Anxiety?* (n.d.). Anxiety.org. https://www.anxiety.org/what-is-anxiety.

10. What to do when someone is at risk. (n.d.). American Foundation for Suicide Prevention. https://afsp.org/what-to-do-when-someone-is-at-risk.

11. National Alliance on Mental Illness. https://nami.org

Disclaimer: Websites may change content as more information becomes available or discovered. There are also instances where a URL (Universal Resource Locator) changes if the owner moves their content to a new site. At the time of publishing, the sources cited on this book were current and relevant to the subject. Please make sure to continue researching and finding ways to make your life healthier in all aspects.

Made in the USA
Monee, IL
02 April 2023

31086513R00056